# KYRG COOKBOOK

## Traditional Recipes from Kyrgyzstan

LIAM LUXE

# CONTENTS

# INTRODUCTION

Kyrgyz food is a mix of traditions, with flavors influenced by the nomads, the Silk Road, and the local farms. The recipes you'll find here are like stories passed down through families, and they show how Kyrgyz people celebrate their culture through food.
You'll find everything from yummy appetizers to delicious desserts. The recipes are easy to follow, so whether you're a kitchen pro or just getting started, you can enjoy the tastes of Kyrgyzstan at home.
Happy cooking!

# APPETIZERS AND SNACKS

## SAMSA (MEAT-FILLED PASTRY)

- **Servings:** 4
- **Time:** 1 hour

**Ingredients:**

- 1 pound ground lamb or beef
- 1 onion, finely chopped
- 2 teaspoons ground cumin
- Salt and pepper to taste
- 1 pack of ready-made puff pastry sheets
- 1 egg (for egg wash)

**Instructions:**

1. Preheat your oven to 375°F (190°C).
2. In a bowl, mix the ground meat, chopped onion, cumin, salt, and pepper.
3. Roll out the puff pastry sheets and cut them into squares.
4. Place a spoonful of the meat mixture onto each pastry square.
5. Fold the pastry over the filling to form a triangle and seal the edges.
6. Beat the egg and brush it over the pastry for a golden finish.
7. Place the samosas on a baking sheet and bake for 20-25 minutes or until golden brown.
8. Allow them to cool slightly before serving.

# LAGMAN SAMSA (LAMB AND NOODLE PASTRY)

- **Servings:** 4
- **Time:** 1 hour and 15 minutes

**Ingredients:**

- 1 pound ground lamb
- 1 onion, finely chopped
- 2 carrots, julienned
- 1 bell pepper, thinly sliced
- 2 cloves garlic, minced
- 1 teaspoon ground cumin
- Salt and pepper to taste
- 1 pack of ready-made puff pastry sheets
- 1 cup cooked and drained noodles (such as egg noodles)
- 1 egg (for egg wash)

**Instructions:**

1. Preheat your oven to 375°F (190°C).
2. In a pan, brown the ground lamb over medium heat. Add chopped onion, julienned carrots, sliced bell pepper, and minced garlic. Cook until vegetables are tender.
3. Season the mixture with ground cumin, salt, and pepper. Stir in the cooked and drained noodles.
4. Roll out the puff pastry sheets and cut them into squares.
5. Spoon the lamb and noodle mixture onto each pastry square.
6. Fold the pastry over the filling to create a triangle and seal the edges.
7. Beat the egg and brush it over the pastry for a golden finish.
8. Place the samsas on a baking sheet and bake for 25-30 minutes or until golden brown.
9. Allow them to cool slightly before serving.

# MANTI (DUMPLINGS FILLED WITH MEAT AND ONIONS)

- **Servings:** 4
- **Time:** 1 hour and 30 minutes

**Ingredients:**

- 1 pound ground beef or lamb
- 1 onion, finely chopped
- 2 cloves garlic, minced
- 1 teaspoon ground cumin
- Salt and pepper to taste

- 1 pack of dumpling wrappers (store-bought or homemade)
- 2 tablespoons vegetable oil
- Yogurt for serving (optional)

**Instructions:**

1. In a bowl, combine the ground meat, chopped onion, minced garlic, ground cumin, salt, and pepper.
2. Lay out the dumpling wrappers on a clean surface.
3. Place a small spoonful of the meat mixture in the center of each wrapper.
4. Fold the wrappers in half, creating a semi-circle, and seal the edges by pressing with your fingers.
5. Bring the two corners of the semi-circle together, creating a hat-like shape, and press to seal.
6. Repeat until all wrappers are filled.
7. Bring a large pot of salted water to a boil.
8. Steam the dumplings in a steamer basket over the boiling water for 20-25 minutes, or until the wrappers are cooked through.
9. While the dumplings are steaming, heat vegetable oil in a pan over medium heat.
10. Once the dumplings are done, transfer them to the pan and lightly fry until the bottoms are golden brown.
11. Serve hot, optionally with yogurt on the side.

# KUURDAK (FRIED MEAT AND POTATOES)

- **Servings:** 4
- **Time:** 1 hour

**Ingredients:**

- 1 pound lamb or beef, diced
- 4 potatoes, peeled and diced
- 1 onion, finely chopped
- 2 cloves garlic, minced
- Salt and pepper to taste
- 2 tablespoons vegetable oil
- Fresh cilantro or parsley for garnish (optional)

**Instructions:**

1. In a large pan, heat vegetable oil over medium-high heat.
2. Add diced meat to the pan and cook until browned.
3. Stir in chopped onion and minced garlic. Cook until the onion is translucent.
4. Add diced potatoes to the pan, mixing them well with the meat and onion.
5. Season with salt and pepper to taste.
6. Cover the pan and let it cook on medium heat for 30-40 minutes, stirring occasionally, until the potatoes are tender and the meat is fully cooked.
7. Once the potatoes are golden brown, and the meat is cooked through, remove the cover and let it fry for an additional 10 minutes to get a nice crust.
8. Garnish with fresh cilantro or parsley if desired.

## KYRGYZ SHORPO (MEAT SOUP)

- **Servings:** 6
- **Time:** 1 hour and 30 minutes

**Ingredients:**

- 1 pound lamb or beef, cut into chunks

- 1 onion, finely chopped
- 2 carrots, sliced
- 2 potatoes, peeled and diced
- 1 turnip, peeled and diced
- 2 tomatoes, chopped
- 4 cloves garlic, minced
- 1 teaspoon ground cumin
- Salt and pepper to taste
- Fresh dill for garnish

## Instructions:

1. In a large pot, combine the meat, chopped onion, sliced carrots, diced potatoes, diced turnip, chopped tomatoes, minced garlic, and ground cumin.
2. Add enough water to cover the ingredients and bring the mixture to a boil.
3. Once boiling, reduce the heat to simmer and let it cook for about 1 hour until the meat is tender and flavors meld.
4. Season the soup with salt and pepper to taste.
5. Garnish with fresh dill before serving.

# BESHBARMAK (BOILED MEAT WITH PASTA)

- **Servings:** 6
- **Time:** 2 hours

## Ingredients:

- 2 pounds lamb or beef, cut into large pieces
- 1 onion, halved

- 4 carrots, halved
- 4 potatoes, peeled and halved
- 1 pack of flat egg noodles
- Salt to taste
- Fresh parsley for garnish

**Instructions:**

1. In a large pot, place the meat, halved onion, halved carrots, and peeled potatoes.
2. Add enough water to cover the ingredients and bring to a boil.
3. Reduce the heat to simmer and cook for about 1.5 to 2 hours, until the meat is tender and the vegetables are cooked through.
4. While the meat is cooking, prepare the egg noodles according to the package instructions. Drain and set aside.
5. Once the meat is done, remove it from the pot and set aside.
6. Arrange cooked noodles on a serving platter.
7. Place the boiled meat, carrots, and potatoes on top of the noodles.
8. Sprinkle with salt to taste.
9. Garnish with fresh parsley.

## SHASHLIK (GRILLED MEAT SKEWERS)

- **Servings:** 4
- **Time:** 1 hour (plus marinating time)

**Ingredients:**

- 1.5 pounds lamb or beef, cubed
- 1 onion, finely chopped
- 2 cloves garlic, minced
- 2 tablespoons olive oil
- 1 teaspoon ground cumin
- 1 teaspoon paprika
- Salt and pepper to taste
- Wooden or metal skewers

**Instructions:**

1. In a bowl, mix together the cubed meat, chopped onion, minced garlic, olive oil, ground cumin, paprika, salt, and pepper.
2. Cover and marinate in the refrigerator for at least 1 hour, or preferably overnight.
3. If using wooden skewers, soak them in water for about 30 minutes to prevent burning.
4. Preheat the grill or grill pan to medium-high heat.
5. Thread the marinated meat onto skewers, alternating with any desired vegetables.
6. Grill the skewers for about 10-15 minutes, turning occasionally, until the meat is cooked to your liking and has a nice char.
7. Remove from the grill and let them rest for a few minutes.

# ASHLYAMFU (COLD NOODLE SALAD)

- **Servings:** 4
- **Time:** 30 minutes (plus chilling time)

**Ingredients:**

- 8 oz cellophane noodles (mung bean or glass noodles)
- 1 cucumber, julienned
- 1 carrot, julienned
- 1 bell pepper, thinly sliced
- 2 green onions, chopped
- 1/4 cup soy sauce
- 2 tablespoons rice vinegar
- 1 tablespoon sesame oil
- 1 tablespoon sugar
- 1 teaspoon red pepper flakes (optional)
- Sesame seeds for garnish (optional)

**Instructions:**

1. Cook the cellophane noodles according to the package instructions. Drain and rinse with cold water.
2. In a large bowl, combine the cooked noodles, julienned cucumber, julienned carrot, sliced bell pepper, and chopped green onions.
3. In a small bowl, whisk together soy sauce, rice vinegar, sesame oil, sugar, and red pepper flakes (if using).
4. Pour the dressing over the noodle mixture and toss until well combined.
5. Cover the bowl and refrigerate for at least 1 hour to allow the flavors to meld.
6. Before serving, toss the salad again to coat the noodles in the dressing.
7. Garnish with sesame seeds if desired.

# CHUCHUK SALAD (TOMATO AND HERB SALAD)

- **Servings:** 4
- **Time:** 15 minutes

**Ingredients:**

- 4 large tomatoes, diced
- 1 cucumber, diced
- 1 red onion, finely chopped
- 1 bunch fresh cilantro, chopped
- 1 bunch fresh mint, chopped
- 2 tablespoons olive oil
- Juice of 1 lemon
- Salt and pepper to taste

**Instructions:**

1. In a large bowl, combine diced tomatoes, diced cucumber, finely chopped red onion, chopped cilantro, and chopped mint.
2. In a small bowl, whisk together olive oil and lemon juice.
3. Pour the dressing over the salad and toss until well combined.
4. Season with salt and pepper to taste.
5. Serve immediately or refrigerate for a short time to let the flavors mingle.

# OROMO (STEAMED MEAT AND VEGETABLE DUMPLINGS)

- **Servings:** 4
- **Time:** 1 hour

**Ingredients:**

- 1/2 pound ground lamb or beef
- 1 cup finely chopped cabbage
- 1 carrot, grated
- 1 onion, finely chopped
- 2 cloves garlic, minced
- 1 teaspoon ground cumin
- Salt and pepper to taste
- Wonton or dumpling wrappers

**Instructions:**

1. In a bowl, combine the ground meat, chopped cabbage, grated carrot, chopped onion, minced garlic, ground cumin, salt, and pepper.
2. Place a small spoonful of the meat and vegetable mixture onto each wonton or dumpling wrapper.
3. Moisten the edges of the wrapper with water and fold it in half, creating a triangle. Press the edges to seal.
4. Repeat until all wrappers are filled.
5. Place the dumplings in a steamer basket lined with parchment paper.
6. Steam for approximately 15-20 minutes or until the dumplings are cooked through.
7. Remove from the steamer and let them cool for a few minutes before serving.

# SOUPS AND STEWS

## KYRGYZ LAGMAN (NOODLE SOUP)

- **Servings:** 6
- **Time:** 1 hour and 30 minutes

**Ingredients:**

- 1 pound lamb or beef, thinly sliced
- 1 onion, thinly sliced
- 2 carrots, julienned
- 1 bell pepper, thinly sliced
- 2 tomatoes, chopped
- 3 cloves garlic, minced
- 1 teaspoon ground cumin
- 1 teaspoon ground coriander
- 1 teaspoon paprika

- Salt and pepper to taste
- 8 cups beef or vegetable broth
- 8 oz lagman or egg noodles
- Fresh cilantro for garnish

**Instructions:**

1. In a large pot, sauté thinly sliced meat until browned.
2. Add sliced onion, julienned carrots, sliced bell pepper, chopped tomatoes, and minced garlic. Cook until vegetables are tender.
3. Season with ground cumin, ground coriander, paprika, salt, and pepper. Stir well.
4. Pour in the broth and bring to a boil. Reduce heat and let it simmer for 30 minutes.
5. In a separate pot, cook lagman or egg noodles according to package instructions. Drain.
6. Add the cooked noodles to the soup and simmer for an additional 10 minutes.
7. Adjust seasoning if necessary and remove from heat.
8. Serve hot, garnished with fresh cilantro.

# SHORPO (LAMB AND VEGETABLE SOUP)

- **Servings:** 6
- **Time:** 2 hours

**Ingredients:**

- 1.5 pounds lamb, cut into chunks
- 1 onion, finely chopped
- 3 carrots, sliced
- 2 potatoes, peeled and diced

- 1 turnip, peeled and diced
- 1 bell pepper, chopped
- 1 cup cabbage, shredded
- 2 tomatoes, chopped
- 3 cloves garlic, minced
- 1 teaspoon ground cumin
- Salt and pepper to taste
- Fresh dill for garnish

**Instructions:**

1. In a large pot, combine lamb, chopped onion, sliced carrots, diced potatoes, diced turnip, chopped bell pepper, shredded cabbage, chopped tomatoes, minced garlic, ground cumin, salt, and pepper.
2. Add enough water to cover the ingredients and bring to a boil.
3. Once boiling, reduce heat to simmer and cook for about 1.5 to 2 hours until the lamb is tender and flavors meld.
4. Season the soup with salt and pepper to taste.
5. Garnish with fresh dill before serving.

## KAZY ISI (STUFFED SAUSAGE)

- **Servings:** 6
- **Time:** 2 hours

**Ingredients:**

- 1 large sausage casing (or synthetic casing)
- 2 pounds lamb, finely minced
- 1 cup rice, cooked
- 1 onion, finely chopped

- 3 cloves garlic, minced
- 1 teaspoon ground black pepper
- 1 teaspoon ground cumin
- Salt to taste

**Instructions:**

1. Rinse the sausage casing thoroughly and soak it in warm water for about 30 minutes.
2. In a bowl, mix finely minced lamb, cooked rice, chopped onion, minced garlic, ground black pepper, ground cumin, and salt.
3. Carefully stuff the sausage casing with the lamb and rice mixture, ensuring it is evenly distributed.
4. Tie off the ends of the sausage casing securely.
5. In a large pot, bring water to a simmer.
6. Gently place the stuffed sausage into the simmering water and cook for about 1.5 to 2 hours.
7. Once cooked, let it cool slightly before slicing.

## KYRGYZ PLOV (RICE PILAF WITH MEAT)

- **Servings:** 6
- **Time:** 1 hour and 30 minutes

**Ingredients:**

- 2 cups basmati rice
- 1 pound lamb or beef, cubed
- 1 large onion, thinly sliced
- 3 carrots, julienned
- 1 cup green peas (fresh or frozen)
- 3 cloves garlic, minced

- 1 teaspoon ground cumin
- 1 teaspoon ground coriander
- Salt and pepper to taste
- 4 cups beef or vegetable broth
- 1/4 cup vegetable oil
- Fresh parsley for garnish

**Instructions:**

1. Rinse the basmati rice under cold water until the water runs clear. Soak the rice in water for 30 minutes, then drain.
2. In a large pot, heat vegetable oil over medium heat. Add cubed meat and brown on all sides.
3. Add thinly sliced onion and cook until translucent.
4. Stir in julienned carrots, green peas, minced garlic, ground cumin, and ground coriander. Cook for a few minutes until the vegetables are slightly tender.
5. Add the drained rice to the pot, stirring gently to combine with the meat and vegetables.
6. Season with salt and pepper to taste.
7. Pour in the broth, bring to a boil, then reduce heat to low. Cover and simmer for about 15-20 minutes, or until the rice is cooked and the liquid is absorbed.
8. Fluff the rice with a fork and let it rest, covered, for an additional 10 minutes.
9. Garnish with fresh parsley before serving.

# CHUCHUK (SAUSAGE AND VEGETABLE STEW)

- **Servings:** 4

- **Time:** 1 hour

**Ingredients:**

- 1 pound smoked sausage, sliced
- 1 onion, finely chopped
- 2 carrots, diced
- 2 potatoes, peeled and diced
- 1 bell pepper, chopped
- 1 cup green beans, chopped
- 2 tomatoes, chopped
- 3 cloves garlic, minced
- 1 teaspoon paprika
- 1 teaspoon ground cumin
- Salt and pepper to taste
- 2 tablespoons vegetable oil
- Fresh parsley for garnish

**Instructions:**

1. In a large pot, heat vegetable oil over medium heat.
2. Add sliced smoked sausage and sauté until lightly browned.
3. Add finely chopped onion and minced garlic, cooking until the onion is translucent.
4. Stir in diced carrots, peeled and diced potatoes, chopped bell pepper, chopped green beans, and chopped tomatoes.
5. Season with paprika, ground cumin, salt, and pepper. Mix well.
6. Cover the pot and simmer for about 30-40 minutes, or until the vegetables are tender.
7. Adjust seasoning if necessary.

8. Garnish with fresh parsley before serving.

# TANDYR NAN (FLATBREAD)

- **Servings:** 8
- **Time:** 2 hours (including resting time)

## Ingredients:

- 4 cups all-purpose flour
- 1 teaspoon salt
- 1 teaspoon sugar
- 1 tablespoon active dry yeast
- 1.5 cups warm water
- 2 tablespoons vegetable oil
- Sesame seeds for sprinkling (optional)

## Instructions:

1. In a bowl, combine warm water, sugar, and active dry yeast. Let it sit for 5-10 minutes until frothy.
2. In a large mixing bowl, combine all-purpose flour and salt.
3. Make a well in the center of the flour mixture and pour in the yeast mixture and vegetable oil.
4. Mix until a dough forms, then knead on a floured surface for about 8-10 minutes until the dough is smooth and elastic.
5. Place the dough in a lightly oiled bowl, cover with a damp cloth, and let it rise in a warm place for 1 hour, or until it doubles in size.
6. Preheat the oven to the highest temperature (usually around 500°F or 260°C) or use a tandoor if available.

7. Punch down the risen dough and divide it into 8 equal portions.
8. Roll each portion into a flat, round shape, about 1/4 inch thick.
9. If using an oven, place the flatbreads on a baking sheet. Optionally, sprinkle sesame seeds on top.
10. Bake for 8-10 minutes or until the flatbreads are golden and puffed up.
11. If using a tandoor, cook the flatbreads until they have a nice char and are cooked through.

# BOSO LAGMAN (FRIED NOODLES WITH MEAT AND VEGETABLES)

- **Servings:** 4
- **Time:** 45 minutes

**Ingredients:**

- 8 oz lagman or egg noodles
- 1/2 pound lamb or beef, thinly sliced
- 1 onion, thinly sliced
- 1 bell pepper, thinly sliced
- 2 carrots, julienned
- 2 tomatoes, chopped
- 3 cloves garlic, minced
- 2 tablespoons vegetable oil
- 2 tablespoons soy sauce
- 1 teaspoon ground cumin
- Salt and pepper to taste
- Fresh cilantro for garnish

**Instructions:**

1. Cook the lagman or egg noodles according to package instructions. Drain and set aside.
2. In a large pan or wok, heat vegetable oil over medium-high heat.
3. Add thinly sliced meat and cook until browned.
4. Stir in thinly sliced onion, julienned carrots, sliced bell pepper, chopped tomatoes, and minced garlic. Cook until the vegetables are tender.
5. Add soy sauce, ground cumin, salt, and pepper. Mix well.
6. Add the cooked noodles to the pan and toss everything together until well combined.
7. Cook for an additional 5-7 minutes, allowing the flavors to meld.
8. Adjust seasoning if necessary.
9. Garnish with fresh cilantro before serving.

# SHORPO YAKHNI (MUTTON BROTH)

- **Servings:** 4
- **Time:** 1 hour and 30 minutes

**Ingredients:**

- 1.5 pounds mutton, cut into chunks
- 1 onion, finely chopped
- 2 carrots, sliced
- 2 potatoes, peeled and diced
- 1 turnip, peeled and diced
- 1 leek, sliced
- 2 tomatoes, chopped
- 3 cloves garlic, minced
- 1 teaspoon ground cumin

- Salt and pepper to taste
- Fresh parsley for garnish

**Instructions:**

1. In a large pot, combine mutton chunks, finely chopped onion, sliced carrots, diced potatoes, diced turnip, sliced leek, chopped tomatoes, minced garlic, ground cumin, salt, and pepper.
2. Add enough water to cover the ingredients and bring to a boil.
3. Once boiling, reduce heat to simmer and let it cook for about 1 to 1.5 hours until the mutton is tender and flavors meld.
4. Season the broth with salt and pepper to taste.
5. Garnish with fresh parsley before serving.

## YRAN (MILK SOUP WITH RICE)

- **Servings:** 4
- **Time:** 40 minutes

**Ingredients:**

- 1 cup rice
- 4 cups whole milk
- 1/4 cup sugar (adjust to taste)
- 1/2 teaspoon vanilla extract
- Pinch of salt
- Ground cinnamon for garnish

**Instructions:**

1. Rinse the rice under cold water until the water runs clear.
2. In a pot, combine the rinsed rice and whole milk.
3. Bring the mixture to a boil over medium heat.
4. Reduce the heat to low and simmer, stirring occasionally, until the rice is cooked and the mixture thickens (about 25-30 minutes).
5. Stir in sugar, vanilla extract, and a pinch of salt. Adjust the sugar to your desired sweetness.
6. Continue to simmer for an additional 5-10 minutes until the sugar is dissolved and the flavors meld.
7. Remove from heat and let it cool slightly.
8. Serve warm, sprinkled with ground cinnamon.

# MAIN DISHES WITH MEAT

## KYRGYZ BESHBARMAK (BOILED MEAT WITH PASTA)

- **Servings:** 6
- **Time:** 2 hours

**Ingredients:**

- 2 pounds lamb or beef, cut into large pieces
- 1 onion, halved
- 4 carrots, halved
- 4 potatoes, peeled and halved
- 1 pack of flat egg noodles
- Salt to taste
- Fresh parsley for garnish

## Instructions:

1. In a large pot, place the meat, halved onion, halved carrots, and peeled, halved potatoes.
2. Add enough water to cover the ingredients and bring to a boil.
3. Reduce the heat to simmer and cook for about 1.5 to 2 hours, until the meat is tender and the vegetables are cooked through.
4. While the meat is cooking, prepare the egg noodles according to the package instructions. Drain and set aside.
5. Once the meat is done, remove it from the pot and set aside.
6. Arrange cooked noodles on a serving platter.
7. Place the boiled meat, carrots, and potatoes on top of the noodles.
8. Sprinkle with salt to taste.
9. Garnish with fresh parsley.

# OROMO (STEAMED MEAT AND VEGETABLE DUMPLINGS)

- **Servings:** 4
- **Time:** 1 hour

## Ingredients:

- 1/2 pound ground lamb or beef
- 1 cup finely chopped cabbage
- 1 carrot, grated
- 1 onion, finely chopped
- 2 cloves garlic, minced

- 1 teaspoon ground cumin
- Salt and pepper to taste
- Wonton or dumpling wrappers

**Instructions:**

1. In a bowl, combine the ground meat, chopped cabbage, grated carrot, chopped onion, minced garlic, ground cumin, salt, and pepper.
2. Place a small spoonful of the meat and vegetable mixture onto each wonton or dumpling wrapper.
3. Moisten the edges of the wrapper with water and fold it in half, creating a triangle. Press the edges to seal.
4. Repeat until all wrappers are filled.
5. Place the dumplings in a steamer basket lined with parchment paper.
6. Steam for approximately 15-20 minutes or until the dumplings are cooked through.
7. Remove from the steamer and let them cool for a few minutes before serving.

## KUURDAK (FRIED MEAT AND POTATOES)

- **Servings:** 4
- **Time:** 1 hour

**Ingredients:**

- 1 pound lamb or beef, diced
- 4 potatoes, peeled and diced
- 1 onion, finely chopped
- 2 cloves garlic, minced
- Salt and pepper to taste

- 2 tablespoons vegetable oil
- Fresh cilantro or parsley for garnish (optional)

**Instructions:**

1. In a large pan, heat vegetable oil over medium-high heat.
2. Add diced meat to the pan and cook until browned.
3. Stir in chopped onion and minced garlic. Cook until the onion is translucent.
4. Add diced potatoes to the pan, mixing them well with the meat and onion.
5. Season with salt and pepper to taste.
6. Cover the pan and let it cook on medium heat for 30-40 minutes, stirring occasionally, until the potatoes are tender and the meat is fully cooked.
7. Once the potatoes are golden brown, and the meat is cooked through, remove the cover and let it fry for an additional 10 minutes to get a nice crust.
8. Garnish with fresh cilantro or parsley if desired.

# LAGMAN (NOODLE DISH WITH MEAT AND VEGETABLES)

- **Servings:** 4
- **Time:** 1 hour and 30 minutes

**Ingredients:**

- 1 pound lamb or beef, thinly sliced
- 8 oz lagman or egg noodles
- 2 tablespoons vegetable oil
- 1 onion, thinly sliced
- 2 carrots, julienned

- 1 bell pepper, thinly sliced
- 1 zucchini, thinly sliced
- 3 tomatoes, chopped
- 3 cloves garlic, minced
- 1 teaspoon ground cumin
- 1 teaspoon paprika
- Salt and pepper to taste
- Fresh cilantro for garnish

## Instructions:

1. Cook the lagman or egg noodles according to the package instructions. Drain and set aside.
2. In a large pan or wok, heat vegetable oil over medium-high heat.
3. Add thinly sliced meat and cook until browned.
4. Stir in thinly sliced onion, julienned carrots, sliced bell pepper, thinly sliced zucchini, chopped tomatoes, and minced garlic. Cook until the vegetables are tender.
5. Add ground cumin, paprika, salt, and pepper. Mix well.
6. Add the cooked noodles to the pan and toss everything together until well combined.
7. Cook for an additional 5-7 minutes, allowing the flavors to meld.
8. Adjust seasoning if necessary.
9. Garnish with fresh cilantro before serving.

# KYRGYZ PLOV (RICE PILAF WITH MEAT)

- **Servings:** 6
- **Time:** 1 hour and 30 minutes

## Ingredients:

- 2 cups basmati rice
- 1 pound lamb or beef, cubed
- 1 large onion, thinly sliced
- 3 carrots, julienned
- 1 cup green peas (fresh or frozen)
- 3 cloves garlic, minced
- 1 teaspoon ground cumin
- 1 teaspoon ground coriander
- Salt and pepper to taste
- 4 cups beef or vegetable broth
- 1/4 cup vegetable oil
- Fresh parsley for garnish

## Instructions:

1. Rinse the basmati rice under cold water until the water runs clear. Soak the rice in water for 30 minutes, then drain.
2. In a large pot, heat vegetable oil over medium heat. Add cubed meat and brown on all sides.
3. Add thinly sliced onion and cook until translucent.
4. Stir in julienned carrots, green peas, minced garlic, ground cumin, and ground coriander. Cook for a few minutes until the vegetables are slightly tender.
5. Add the drained rice to the pot, stirring gently to combine with the meat and vegetables.
6. Season with salt and pepper to taste.
7. Pour in the broth, bring to a boil, then reduce heat to low. Cover and simmer for about 15-20 minutes, or until the rice is cooked and the liquid is absorbed.
8. Fluff the rice with a fork and let it rest, covered, for an additional 10 minutes.
9. Garnish with fresh parsley before serving.

# CHUCHUK (SAUSAGE AND VEGETABLE STEW)

- **Servings:** 4
- **Time:** 1 hour

## Ingredients:

- 1 pound smoked sausage, sliced
- 1 onion, finely chopped
- 2 carrots, diced
- 2 potatoes, peeled and diced
- 1 bell pepper, chopped
- 1 cup green beans, chopped
- 2 tomatoes, chopped
- 3 cloves garlic, minced
- 1 teaspoon paprika
- 1 teaspoon ground cumin
- Salt and pepper to taste
- 2 tablespoons vegetable oil
- Fresh parsley for garnish

## Instructions:

1. In a large pot, heat vegetable oil over medium heat.
2. Add sliced smoked sausage and sauté until lightly browned.
3. Add finely chopped onion and minced garlic, cooking until the onion is translucent.
4. Stir in diced carrots, peeled and diced potatoes, chopped bell pepper, chopped green beans, and chopped tomatoes.

5. Season with paprika, ground cumin, salt, and pepper. Mix well.
6. Cover the pot and simmer for about 30-40 minutes, or until the vegetables are tender.
7. Adjust seasoning if necessary.
8. Garnish with fresh parsley before serving.

# KAZY ISI (STUFFED SAUSAGE)

- **Servings:** 6
- **Time:** 2 hours

## Ingredients:

- 1 large sausage casing (or synthetic casing)
- 2 pounds lamb, finely minced
- 1 cup rice, cooked
- 1 onion, finely chopped
- 3 cloves garlic, minced
- 1 teaspoon ground black pepper
- 1 teaspoon ground cumin
- Salt to taste

## Instructions:

1. Rinse the sausage casing thoroughly and soak it in warm water for about 30 minutes.
2. In a bowl, mix finely minced lamb, cooked rice, chopped onion, minced garlic, ground black pepper, ground cumin, and salt.
3. Carefully stuff the sausage casing with the lamb and rice mixture, ensuring it is evenly distributed.
4. Tie off the ends of the sausage casing securely.

5. In a large pot, bring water to a simmer.
6. Gently place the stuffed sausage into the simmering water and cook for about 1.5 to 2 hours.
7. Once cooked, let it cool slightly before slicing.

# BESHBARMAK WITH KAZY (BOILED MEAT WITH SAUSAGE)

- **Servings:** 6
- **Time:** 2 hours

**Ingredients:**

- 2 pounds lamb or beef, cut into large pieces
- 1 pound kazy (dried horse sausage), sliced
- 1 onion, halved
- 4 carrots, halved
- 4 potatoes, peeled and halved
- 1 pack of flat egg noodles
- Salt to taste
- Fresh parsley for garnish

**Instructions:**

1. In a large pot, place the lamb or beef, kazy slices, halved onion, halved carrots, and peeled, halved potatoes.
2. Add enough water to cover the ingredients and bring to a boil.
3. Reduce the heat to simmer and cook for about 1.5 to 2 hours until the meat is tender and the vegetables are cooked through.

4. While the meat is cooking, prepare the egg noodles according to the package instructions. Drain and set aside.
5. Once the meat is done, remove it from the pot and set aside.
6. Arrange cooked noodles on a serving platter.
7. Place the boiled meat, kazy slices, carrots, and potatoes on top of the noodles.
8. Sprinkle with salt to taste.
9. Garnish with fresh parsley.

# BESHBARMAK WITH ZHAYA (BOILED MEAT WITH LIVER)

- **Servings:** 6
- **Time:** 2 hours

**Ingredients:**

- 2 pounds lamb or beef, cut into large pieces
- 1 pound beef liver, sliced
- 1 onion, halved
- 4 carrots, halved
- 4 potatoes, peeled and halved
- 1 pack of flat egg noodles
- Salt to taste
- Fresh parsley for garnish

**Instructions:**

1. In a large pot, place the lamb or beef, sliced beef liver, halved onion, halved carrots, and peeled, halved potatoes.

2. Add enough water to cover the ingredients and bring to a boil.
3. Reduce the heat to simmer and cook for about 1.5 to 2 hours until the meat is tender and the vegetables are cooked through.
4. While the meat is cooking, prepare the egg noodles according to the package instructions. Drain and set aside.
5. Once the meat is done, remove it from the pot and set aside.
6. Arrange cooked noodles on a serving platter.
7. Place the boiled meat, sliced liver, carrots, and potatoes on top of the noodles.
8. Sprinkle with salt to taste.
9. Garnish with fresh parsley.

## SHASHLIK (GRILLED MEAT SKEWERS)

- **Servings:** 4
- **Time:** 1 hour (plus marinating time)

**Ingredients:**

- 2 pounds lamb or beef, cut into 1-inch cubes
- 1 onion, finely chopped
- 3 cloves garlic, minced
- 1/4 cup vegetable oil
- 1/4 cup red wine vinegar
- 1 teaspoon ground cumin
- 1 teaspoon paprika
- Salt and pepper to taste
- Metal or wooden skewers (if using wooden skewers, soak them in water for 30 minutes)

## Instructions:

1. In a bowl, mix finely chopped onion, minced garlic, vegetable oil, red wine vinegar, ground cumin, paprika, salt, and pepper to create the marinade.
2. Place the meat cubes in the marinade, ensuring they are well coated. Cover and refrigerate for at least 4 hours, preferably overnight.
3. Preheat the grill to medium-high heat.
4. Thread the marinated meat cubes onto skewers.
5. Grill the skewers for about 10-15 minutes, turning occasionally, until the meat is cooked to your desired level of doneness.
6. Remove from the grill and let the skewers rest for a few minutes.

# VEGETARIAN DELIGHTS

## DIMLAMA (VEGETABLE STEW)

- **Servings:** 6
- **Time:** 2 hours

**Ingredients:**

- 1 pound lamb or beef, cubed
- 1 onion, thinly sliced
- 3 potatoes, peeled and diced
- 2 carrots, sliced
- 1 bell pepper, chopped
- 1 zucchini, sliced
- 1 eggplant, diced
- 3 tomatoes, chopped
- 3 cloves garlic, minced

- 1 teaspoon ground cumin
- 1 teaspoon paprika
- Salt and pepper to taste
- 1 cup water
- Fresh dill for garnish

**Instructions:**

1. In a large pot, layer the cubed meat at the bottom.
2. Add thinly sliced onion, diced potatoes, sliced carrots, chopped bell pepper, sliced zucchini, diced eggplant, chopped tomatoes, and minced garlic.
3. Sprinkle ground cumin, paprika, salt, and pepper evenly over the layers.
4. Pour 1 cup of water over the ingredients.
5. Cover the pot and bring it to a boil over medium heat.
6. Once boiling, reduce heat to low and simmer for about 1.5 to 2 hours until the meat is tender and the vegetables are cooked through.
7. Adjust seasoning if necessary.
8. Garnish with fresh dill before serving.

## LAGMAN (VEGETARIAN NOODLE DISH)

- **Servings:** 4
- **Time:** 1 hour and 30 minutes

**Ingredients:**

- 8 oz lagman or egg noodles
- 2 tablespoons vegetable oil
- 1 onion, thinly sliced
- 2 carrots, julienned

- 1 bell pepper, thinly sliced
- 1 zucchini, thinly sliced
- 1 cup green beans, chopped
- 3 tomatoes, chopped
- 3 cloves garlic, minced
- 1 teaspoon ground cumin
- 1 teaspoon paprika
- Salt and pepper to taste
- Fresh cilantro for garnish

**Instructions:**

1. Cook the lagman or egg noodles according to the package instructions. Drain and set aside.
2. In a large pan or wok, heat vegetable oil over medium-high heat.
3. Add thinly sliced onion and cook until translucent.
4. Stir in julienned carrots, sliced bell pepper, thinly sliced zucchini, chopped green beans, chopped tomatoes, and minced garlic. Cook until the vegetables are tender.
5. Add ground cumin, paprika, salt, and pepper. Mix well.
6. Add the cooked noodles to the pan and toss everything together until well combined.
7. Cook for an additional 5-7 minutes, allowing the flavors to meld.
8. Adjust seasoning if necessary.
9. Garnish with fresh cilantro before serving.

# TANDYR NAN (FLATBREAD)

- **Servings:** 8
- **Time:** 2 hours (including resting time)

## Ingredients:

- 4 cups all-purpose flour
- 1 teaspoon salt
- 1 teaspoon sugar
- 1 tablespoon active dry yeast
- 1.5 cups warm water
- 2 tablespoons vegetable oil
- Sesame seeds for sprinkling (optional)

## Instructions:

1. In a bowl, combine warm water, sugar, and active dry yeast. Let it sit for 5-10 minutes until frothy.
2. In a large mixing bowl, combine all-purpose flour and salt.
3. Make a well in the center of the flour mixture and pour in the yeast mixture and vegetable oil.
4. Mix until a dough forms, then knead on a floured surface for about 8-10 minutes until the dough is smooth and elastic.
5. Place the dough in a lightly oiled bowl, cover with a damp cloth, and let it rise in a warm place for 1 hour, or until it doubles in size.
6. Preheat the oven to the highest temperature (usually around 500°F or 260°C) or use a tandoor if available.
7. Punch down the risen dough and divide it into 8 equal portions.
8. Roll each portion into a flat, round shape, about 1/4 inch thick.
9. If using an oven, place the flatbreads on a baking sheet. Optionally, sprinkle sesame seeds on top.

10. Bake for 8-10 minutes or until the flatbreads are golden and puffed up.
11. If using a tandoor, cook the flatbreads until they have a nice char and are cooked through.

# UYGHUR SOMSA (VEGETARIAN PASTRY)

- **Servings:** 6
- **Time:** 1 hour

**Ingredients:**

- 2 cups all-purpose flour
- 1/2 cup warm water
- 2 tablespoons vegetable oil
- 1 teaspoon salt
- 1 large potato, grated
- 1 carrot, grated
- 1 onion, finely chopped
- 1/2 cup cabbage, finely shredded
- 2 tablespoons vegetable oil (for sautéing)
- 1 teaspoon ground cumin
- Salt and pepper to taste

**Instructions:**

1. In a large bowl, combine flour, warm water, vegetable oil, and salt. Knead the mixture into a smooth dough. Cover and let it rest for 30 minutes.
2. In a pan, heat 2 tablespoons of vegetable oil over medium heat. Add chopped onions and sauté until translucent.
3. Add grated potato, grated carrot, and finely shredded cabbage to the pan. Cook until the vegetables are tender.

4. Season the vegetable mixture with ground cumin, salt, and pepper. Mix well.
5. Preheat the oven to 375°F (190°C).
6. Divide the dough into 6 equal portions. Roll each portion into a thin, oval-shaped disk.
7. Place a generous portion of the vegetable filling on one half of each dough disk.
8. Fold the other half of the dough over the filling, creating a semi-circle shape. Seal the edges by pressing them together.
9. Place the filled pastries on a baking sheet and bake for 20-25 minutes, or until they are golden brown.
10. Remove from the oven and let them cool slightly before serving.

# DYMDAMA (VEGETABLE STEW WITH PUMPKIN)

- **Servings:** 4
- **Time:** 1 hour

**Ingredients:**

- 2 cups pumpkin, peeled and diced
- 2 potatoes, peeled and diced
- 2 carrots, sliced
- 1 onion, finely chopped
- 1 bell pepper, chopped
- 2 tomatoes, chopped
- 1 cup green beans, chopped
- 3 cloves garlic, minced
- 1/4 cup vegetable oil

- 1 teaspoon ground coriander
- 1 teaspoon paprika
- Salt and pepper to taste
- Fresh cilantro for garnish

**Instructions:**

1. In a large pot, heat vegetable oil over medium heat.
2. Add finely chopped onion and minced garlic. Sauté until the onion is translucent.
3. Add diced pumpkin, diced potatoes, sliced carrots, chopped bell pepper, chopped tomatoes, and chopped green beans to the pot.
4. Season with ground coriander, paprika, salt, and pepper. Mix well.
5. Cover the pot and let it simmer for about 30-40 minutes, or until the vegetables are tender.
6. Adjust seasoning if necessary.
7. Garnish with fresh cilantro before serving.

# KYRGYZ PLOV (VEGETARIAN RICE PILAF)

- **Servings:** 6
- **Time:** 1 hour

**Ingredients:**

- 2 cups basmati rice
- 1 large onion, thinly sliced
- 3 carrots, julienned
- 1 cup green peas (fresh or frozen)
- 3 cloves garlic, minced
- 1 teaspoon ground cumin

- 1 teaspoon ground coriander
- Salt and pepper to taste
- 4 cups vegetable broth
- 1/4 cup vegetable oil
- Fresh parsley for garnish

**Instructions:**

1. Rinse the basmati rice under cold water until the water runs clear. Soak the rice in water for 30 minutes, then drain.
2. In a large pot, heat vegetable oil over medium heat. Add thinly sliced onion and cook until translucent.
3. Stir in julienned carrots, green peas, minced garlic, ground cumin, and ground coriander. Cook for a few minutes until the vegetables are slightly tender.
4. Add the drained rice to the pot, stirring gently to combine with the vegetables.
5. Season with salt and pepper to taste.
6. Pour in the vegetable broth, bring to a boil, then reduce heat to low. Cover and simmer for about 15-20 minutes, or until the rice is cooked and the liquid is absorbed.
7. Fluff the rice with a fork and let it rest, covered, for an additional 10 minutes.
8. Garnish with fresh parsley before serving.

# YRAN (VEGETARIAN MILK SOUP WITH RICE)

- **Servings:** 4
- **Time:** 40 minutes

**Ingredients:**

- 1 cup rice
- 4 cups whole milk
- 1/4 cup sugar (adjust to taste)
- 1/2 teaspoon vanilla extract
- Pinch of salt
- Ground cinnamon for garnish

**Instructions:**

1. Rinse the rice under cold water until the water runs clear.
2. In a pot, combine the rinsed rice and whole milk.
3. Bring the mixture to a boil over medium heat.
4. Reduce the heat to low and simmer, stirring occasionally, until the rice is cooked and the mixture thickens (about 25-30 minutes).
5. Stir in sugar, vanilla extract, and a pinch of salt. Adjust the sugar to your desired sweetness.
6. Continue to simmer for an additional 5-10 minutes until the sugar is dissolved and the flavors meld.
7. Remove from heat and let it cool slightly.
8. Serve warm, sprinkled with ground cinnamon.

# CHUCHUK SALAD (TOMATO AND HERB SALAD)

- **Servings:** 4
- **Time:** 15 minutes

**Ingredients:**

- 4 large tomatoes, diced
- 1 cucumber, diced
- 1 red onion, finely chopped

- 1 bunch fresh cilantro, chopped
- 1 bunch fresh mint, chopped
- 1 bunch fresh parsley, chopped
- 1 lemon, juiced
- 3 tablespoons olive oil
- Salt and pepper to taste

## Instructions:

1. In a large bowl, combine diced tomatoes, diced cucumber, finely chopped red onion, chopped cilantro, chopped mint, and chopped parsley.
2. In a small bowl, whisk together lemon juice and olive oil to create the dressing.
3. Pour the dressing over the salad and toss gently to coat.
4. Season with salt and pepper to taste.
5. Let the salad sit for a few minutes to allow the flavors to meld.
6. Serve chilled.

# JENT (BUCKWHEAT PORRIDGE)

- **Servings:** 4
- **Time:** 30 minutes

## Ingredients:

- 1 cup buckwheat groats
- 2 cups water
- 2 cups milk (dairy or plant-based)
- 2 tablespoons butter
- Salt to taste
- Honey or maple syrup for serving (optional)

## Instructions:

1. Rinse the buckwheat groats under cold water.
2. In a saucepan, combine the rinsed buckwheat with 2 cups of water. Bring to a boil.
3. Reduce the heat to low, cover, and simmer for 15 minutes or until the water is absorbed and the buckwheat is tender.
4. In a separate pot, heat the milk until warm but not boiling.
5. Add the warm milk to the cooked buckwheat, stirring continuously.
6. Allow the mixture to simmer for an additional 10-15 minutes, stirring occasionally.
7. Add butter and salt to taste, stirring until the butter is melted.
8. Remove from heat and let it rest for a few minutes before serving.
9. Serve hot, drizzled with honey or maple syrup if desired.

## KESME (VEGETARIAN NOODLE DISH)

- **Servings:** 4
- **Time:** 30 minutes

## Ingredients:

- 8 oz kesme noodles or egg noodles
- 2 tablespoons vegetable oil
- 1 onion, thinly sliced
- 2 carrots, julienned
- 1 bell pepper, thinly sliced
- 1 zucchini, thinly sliced

- 1 cup green beans, chopped
- 3 tomatoes, chopped
- 3 cloves garlic, minced
- 1 teaspoon ground cumin
- 1 teaspoon paprika
- Salt and pepper to taste
- Fresh cilantro for garnish

**Instructions:**

1. Cook the kesme noodles or egg noodles according to the package instructions. Drain and set aside.
2. In a large pan or wok, heat vegetable oil over medium-high heat.
3. Add thinly sliced onion and cook until translucent.
4. Stir in julienned carrots, sliced bell pepper, thinly sliced zucchini, chopped green beans, chopped tomatoes, and minced garlic. Cook until the vegetables are tender.
5. Add ground cumin, paprika, salt, and pepper. Mix well.
6. Add the cooked noodles to the pan and toss everything together until well combined.
7. Cook for an additional 5-7 minutes, allowing the flavors to meld.
8. Adjust seasoning if necessary.
9. Garnish with fresh cilantro before serving.

# DUMPLINGS AND PASTRIES

## MANTI (DUMPLINGS FILLED WITH MEAT AND ONIONS)

- **Servings:** 4
- **Time:** 2 hours

**Ingredients:** *For the Dough:*

- 2 cups all-purpose flour
- 1/2 cup water
- 1/2 teaspoon salt

*For the Filling:*

- 1/2 pound ground lamb or beef
- 1 onion, finely chopped

- 2 cloves garlic, minced
- Salt and pepper to taste

*For the Sauce:*

- 1/2 cup plain yogurt
- 2 tablespoons butter, melted
- 1 teaspoon paprika
- Fresh parsley for garnish

**Instructions:**

1. In a large bowl, combine flour, water, and salt. Knead the mixture into a smooth dough. Cover and let it rest for 30 minutes.
2. In a mixing bowl, mix ground meat, finely chopped onion, minced garlic, salt, and pepper to create the filling.
3. Roll out the dough on a floured surface into a thin sheet.
4. Cut the sheet into small squares (about 2 inches by 2 inches).
5. Place a small spoonful of the meat filling in the center of each square.
6. Fold the squares into a triangle, sealing the edges tightly.
7. Place the prepared Manti in a steamer basket, ensuring they are not touching each other.
8. Steam for approximately 30-40 minutes or until the dumplings are cooked through.
9. While the Manti are steaming, prepare the sauce by mixing yogurt with melted butter and paprika.
10. Once the Manti are ready, serve them hot, drizzled with the yogurt sauce, and garnished with fresh parsley.

# SAMSA (MEAT-FILLED PASTRY)

- **Servings:** 6
- **Time:** 1 hour and 30 minutes

**Ingredients:** *For the Dough:*

- 3 cups all-purpose flour
- 1 cup water
- 1/2 cup vegetable oil
- 1/2 teaspoon salt

*For the Filling:*

- 1 pound ground lamb or beef
- 1 onion, finely chopped
- 2 cloves garlic, minced
- 1 teaspoon ground cumin
- 1 teaspoon ground coriander
- Salt and pepper to taste

**Instructions:** *For the Dough:*

1. In a large bowl, combine flour, water, vegetable oil, and salt. Knead the mixture into a soft, elastic dough. Cover and let it rest for 30 minutes.

*For the Filling:* 2. In a mixing bowl, combine ground meat, finely chopped onion, minced garlic, ground cumin, ground coriander, salt, and pepper.

*Assembling the Samsa:* 3. Preheat the oven to 375°F (190°C).

4. Divide the dough into small balls, and roll each ball into a thin oval shape.

5. Place a generous spoonful of the meat filling onto one half of the oval-shaped dough.
6. Fold the other half of the dough over the filling, creating a triangle shape. Press the edges to seal.
7. Place the prepared Samsa on a baking sheet.
8. Bake for 25-30 minutes or until the pastry is golden brown.

# LAGMAN SAMSA (LAMB AND NOODLE PASTRY)

- **Servings:** 6
- **Time:** 2 hours

**Ingredients:** *For the Dough:*

- 3 cups all-purpose flour
- 1 cup water
- 1/2 cup vegetable oil
- 1/2 teaspoon salt

*For the Filling:*

- 1 pound ground lamb
- 1 onion, finely chopped
- 2 cloves garlic, minced
- 1 cup cooked lagman or egg noodles
- 1 teaspoon ground cumin
- 1 teaspoon ground coriander
- Salt and pepper to taste

**Instructions:** *For the Dough:*

1. In a large bowl, combine flour, water, vegetable oil, and salt. Knead the mixture into a soft, elastic dough. Cover and let it rest for 30 minutes.

*For the Filling:* 2. In a mixing bowl, combine ground lamb, finely chopped onion, minced garlic, cooked lagman or egg noodles, ground cumin, ground coriander, salt, and pepper.

*Assembling the Lagman Samsa:* 3. Preheat the oven to 375°F (190°C).

4. Divide the dough into small balls and roll each ball into a thin oval shape.
5. Place a generous spoonful of the lamb and noodle filling onto one half of the oval-shaped dough.
6. Fold the other half of the dough over the filling, creating a triangle shape. Press the edges to seal.
7. Place the prepared Lagman Samsa on a baking sheet.
8. Bake for 25-30 minutes or until the pastry is golden brown.

# KYRGYZ BELYASH (FRIED MEAT PIE)

- **Servings:** 6
- **Time:** 2 hours

**Ingredients:** *For the Dough:*

- 3 cups all-purpose flour
- 1 cup warm milk
- 1/4 cup vegetable oil
- 1 tablespoon sugar
- 1 tablespoon active dry yeast

- 1/2 teaspoon salt

*For the Filling:*

- 1 pound ground beef or lamb
- 1 onion, finely chopped
- 2 cloves garlic, minced
- 1 teaspoon ground cumin
- 1 teaspoon ground coriander
- Salt and pepper to taste

**Instructions:** *For the Dough:*

1. In a bowl, combine warm milk, sugar, and active dry yeast. Let it sit for 5-10 minutes until frothy.
2. In a large mixing bowl, combine flour, vegetable oil, salt, and the yeast mixture. Knead into a soft dough. Cover and let it rise for 1 hour.

*For the Filling:* 3. In a skillet, cook ground beef or lamb over medium heat until browned.

4. Add finely chopped onion, minced garlic, ground cumin, ground coriander, salt, and pepper. Cook until the onion is translucent. Remove from heat.

*Assembling the Belyash:* 5. Preheat vegetable oil in a deep fryer or a large, deep pan to 350°F (175°C).

6. Divide the risen dough into small balls.
7. Flatten each ball into a round disc and place a spoonful of the meat filling in the center.
8. Fold the edges of the dough over the filling, creating a sealed pocket.

9. Carefully drop each Belyash into the hot oil and fry until golden brown on both sides.
10. Remove and drain excess oil on paper towels.

# CHIBUREKKI (FRIED PASTRY WITH MEAT)

- **Servings:** 6
- **Time:** 2 hours

**Ingredients:** *For the Dough:*

- 3 cups all-purpose flour
- 1 cup warm water
- 1/4 cup vegetable oil
- 1 tablespoon white vinegar
- 1 teaspoon salt

*For the Filling:*

- 1 pound ground beef or lamb
- 1 onion, finely chopped
- 2 cloves garlic, minced
- 1 teaspoon ground cumin
- 1 teaspoon ground coriander
- Salt and pepper to taste

**Instructions:** *For the Dough:*

1. In a bowl, combine warm water, vegetable oil, vinegar, and salt.
2. Gradually add the flour, kneading until a smooth dough forms. Cover and let it rest for 1 hour.

*For the Filling:* 3. In a skillet, cook ground beef or lamb over medium heat until browned.

4. Add finely chopped onion, minced garlic, ground cumin, ground coriander, salt, and pepper. Cook until the onion is translucent. Remove from heat.

*Assembling the Chiburekki:* 5. Preheat vegetable oil in a deep fryer or a large, deep pan to 350°F (175°C).

6. Divide the rested dough into small balls.
7. Roll out each ball into a thin, round disc.
8. Place a spoonful of the meat filling on one half of the dough circle.
9. Fold the other half over the filling, creating a semi-circle. Press the edges to seal.
10. Carefully drop each Chiburekki into the hot oil and fry until golden brown on both sides.
11. Remove and drain excess oil on paper towels.

## TYIYN ENISH (FLATBREAD WITH CHEESE)

- **Servings:** 4
- **Time:** 1 hour

**Ingredients:** *For the Dough:*

- 2 cups all-purpose flour
- 1 cup warm water
- 2 tablespoons vegetable oil
- 1/2 teaspoon salt

*For the Filling:*

- 1 cup feta cheese, crumbled
- 1 cup mozzarella cheese, shredded
- 1/4 cup fresh parsley, chopped
- 1/4 cup green onions, finely chopped
- Salt and pepper to taste

**Instructions:** *For the Dough:*

1. In a large bowl, combine warm water, vegetable oil, and salt.
2. Gradually add the flour, kneading until a soft, elastic dough forms. Cover and let it rest for 30 minutes.

*For the Filling:* 3. In a mixing bowl, combine crumbled feta cheese, shredded mozzarella cheese, chopped fresh parsley, green onions, salt, and pepper.

*Assembling the Tyiyn Enish:* 4. Preheat the oven to 400°F (200°C).

5. Divide the rested dough into small balls.
6. Roll out each ball into a thin, round disc.
7. Place a generous portion of the cheese filling in the center of each disc.
8. Fold the edges over the filling, creating a sealed pocket.
9. Place the prepared Tyiyn Enish on a baking sheet.
10. Bake for 20-25 minutes or until the bread is golden brown and the cheese is melted.

# KYRGYZ PIROSHKI (STUFFED BREAD ROLLS)

- **Servings:** 6

- **Time:** 2 hours

**Ingredients:** *For the Dough:*

- 3 cups all-purpose flour
- 1 cup warm milk
- 1/4 cup vegetable oil
- 1 tablespoon sugar
- 1 tablespoon active dry yeast
- 1/2 teaspoon salt

*For the Filling:*

- 1 pound ground beef or lamb
- 1 onion, finely chopped
- 2 cloves garlic, minced
- 1 cup cabbage, finely shredded
- 1 carrot, grated
- 1 teaspoon ground cumin
- 1 teaspoon ground coriander
- Salt and pepper to taste

**Instructions:** *For the Dough:*

1. In a bowl, combine warm milk, sugar, and active dry yeast. Let it sit for 5-10 minutes until frothy.
2. In a large mixing bowl, combine flour, vegetable oil, salt, and the yeast mixture. Knead into a soft dough. Cover and let it rise for 1 hour.

*For the Filling:* 3. In a skillet, cook ground beef or lamb over medium heat until browned.

4. Add finely chopped onion, minced garlic, finely shredded cabbage, grated carrot, ground cumin, ground coriander, salt, and pepper. Cook until the vegetables are tender. Remove from heat.

*Assembling the Piroshki:* 5. Preheat the oven to 375°F (190°C).

6. Divide the risen dough into small balls.
7. Roll out each ball into a thin, round disc.
8. Place a spoonful of the meat and vegetable filling on one half of the disc.
9. Fold the other half of the dough over the filling, creating a semi-circle. Press the edges to seal.
10. Place the prepared Piroshki on a baking sheet.
11. Bake for 25-30 minutes or until the bread is golden brown.

# KYRGYZ BORSOK (FRIED DOUGH)

- **Servings:** 6
- **Time:** 1.5 hours

## Ingredients:

- 3 cups all-purpose flour
- 1 cup warm milk
- 1 tablespoon vegetable oil
- 1 tablespoon sugar
- 1 tablespoon active dry yeast
- 1/2 teaspoon salt
- Vegetable oil for frying

## Instructions:

1. In a bowl, combine warm milk, sugar, and active dry yeast. Let it sit for 5-10 minutes until frothy.
2. In a large mixing bowl, combine flour, vegetable oil, salt, and the yeast mixture. Knead into a soft dough. Cover and let it rise for 1 hour.
3. After the dough has risen, heat vegetable oil in a deep fryer or a large, deep pan to 350°F (175°C).
4. Divide the dough into small balls, approximately 1-2 inches in diameter.
5. Roll out each ball into a small disc or shape of your preference.
6. Carefully place the dough into the hot oil and fry until golden brown on both sides, turning as needed.
7. Remove the fried dough with a slotted spoon and place it on paper towels to absorb excess oil.
8. Repeat the process with the remaining dough balls.

# BALISH (FLATBREAD WITH MEAT AND POTATOES)

- **Servings:** 6
- **Time:** 2 hours

**Ingredients:** *For the Dough:*

- 3 cups all-purpose flour
- 1 cup warm water
- 1/4 cup vegetable oil
- 1 tablespoon sugar
- 1 tablespoon active dry yeast
- 1/2 teaspoon salt

*For the Filling:*

- 1/2 pound ground lamb or beef
- 2 potatoes, peeled and diced
- 1 onion, finely chopped
- 2 cloves garlic, minced
- 1 teaspoon ground cumin
- 1 teaspoon ground coriander
- Salt and pepper to taste

**Instructions:** *For the Dough:*

1. In a bowl, combine warm water, sugar, and active dry yeast. Let it sit for 5-10 minutes until frothy.
2. In a large mixing bowl, combine flour, vegetable oil, salt, and the yeast mixture. Knead into a soft dough. Cover and let it rise for 1 hour.

*For the Filling:* 3. In a skillet, cook ground lamb or beef over medium heat until browned.

4. Add finely chopped onion, minced garlic, diced potatoes, ground cumin, ground coriander, salt, and pepper. Cook until the potatoes are tender. Remove from heat.

*Assembling the Balish:* 5. Preheat the oven to 375°F (190°C).

6. Divide the risen dough into small balls.
7. Roll out each ball into a thin, round disc.
8. Place a generous portion of the meat and potato filling on one half of the disc.
9. Fold the other half of the dough over the filling, creating a semi-circle. Press the edges to seal.
10. Place the prepared Balish on a baking sheet.
11. Bake for 25-30 minutes or until the bread is golden brown.

# SWEETS AND DESSERTS

## CHAK-CHAK (FRIED DOUGH WITH HONEY)

- **Servings:** 8
- **Time:** 1.5 hours

**Ingredients:** *For the Dough:*

- 3 cups all-purpose flour
- 3 large eggs
- 1/4 cup unsalted butter, melted
- 1/4 cup sour cream
- 1/4 cup sugar
- 1 teaspoon vanilla extract
- 1/2 teaspoon baking soda
- A pinch of salt

*For the Syrup:*

- 1 cup honey
- 1/4 cup water
- 1 teaspoon lemon juice

**Instructions:** *For the Dough:*

1. In a large bowl, whisk together eggs, melted butter, sour cream, sugar, vanilla extract, baking soda, and a pinch of salt.
2. Gradually add the flour, mixing until a soft dough forms.
3. Knead the dough on a floured surface until smooth. Cover and let it rest for 30 minutes.

*For the Syrup:* 4. In a saucepan, combine honey, water, and lemon juice. Bring to a simmer over medium heat and cook for 5 minutes. Remove from heat and let it cool.

*Assembling Chak-Chak:* 5. Preheat vegetable oil in a deep fryer or a large, deep pan to 350°F (175°C).

6. Divide the rested dough into small balls.
7. Roll out each ball into a thin log or rope shape.
8. Cut the log into small pieces, about 1 inch in length.
9. Fry the dough pieces in batches until golden brown. Remove and drain on paper towels.
10. Once all the dough pieces are fried, transfer them to a large bowl.
11. Pour the cooled honey syrup over the fried dough and gently toss until evenly coated.
12. Allow Chak-Chak to cool and absorb the syrup before serving.

# KURT (DRIED CHEESE BALLS)

- **Servings:** 6
- **Time:** 2 days (including drying time)

## Ingredients:

- 2 cups whole milk
- 1/4 cup plain yogurt
- Salt to taste

## Instructions:

1. In a saucepan, heat the whole milk over medium heat until it reaches a gentle boil.
2. Remove the milk from heat and let it cool until it is warm to the touch.
3. In a small bowl, mix plain yogurt with a couple of tablespoons of the warm milk to create a smooth mixture.
4. Add the yogurt mixture back to the warm milk, stirring well to combine.
5. Cover the saucepan with a lid and let it sit undisturbed for about 4-6 hours, or until the milk has curdled and formed a thick mass.

*Straining the Cheese:* 6. Line a sieve or colander with cheesecloth and place it over a bowl.

7. Pour the curdled milk into the cheesecloth to separate the whey from the curds. Allow it to drain for 2-3 hours.
8. Once most of the whey has drained, gather the cheesecloth and gently squeeze to remove excess liquid.

9. Transfer the cheese mass to a bowl and knead it with a pinch of salt until it becomes smooth and pliable.

*Forming Kurt:* 10. Pinch small portions of the cheese and roll them into small balls, about 1 inch in diameter.

11. Arrange the cheese balls on a tray, ensuring they are not touching.
12. Place the tray in a well-ventilated area and let the cheese balls air-dry for 1-2 days until they become firm and dry.
13. Once dried, store the Kurt in an airtight container at room temperature.

# BESBARMAK (SWEET DUMPLINGS)

- **Servings:** 6
- **Time:** 1.5 hours

**Ingredients:** *For the Dough:*

- 2 cups all-purpose flour
- 1/2 cup warm water
- 2 tablespoons vegetable oil
- 1 tablespoon sugar
- 1 teaspoon active dry yeast
- 1/4 teaspoon salt

*For the Filling:*

- 1 cup sweetened condensed milk
- 1 cup ground nuts (walnuts or almonds)
- 1/4 cup sugar
- 1 teaspoon ground cinnamon

- 1/2 teaspoon vanilla extract

**Instructions:** *For the Dough:*

1. In a bowl, combine warm water, sugar, and active dry yeast. Let it sit for 5-10 minutes until frothy.
2. In a large mixing bowl, combine flour, vegetable oil, salt, and the yeast mixture. Knead into a soft dough. Cover and let it rise for 1 hour.

*For the Filling:* 3. In a separate bowl, mix sweetened condensed milk, ground nuts, sugar, ground cinnamon, and vanilla extract to create the filling.

*Assembling Besbarmak:* 4. Preheat the oven to 375°F (190°C).

5. Divide the risen dough into small balls.
6. Roll out each ball into a thin, round disc.
7. Place a spoonful of the sweetened nut filling on one half of the disc.
8. Fold the other half of the dough over the filling, creating a semi-circle. Press the edges to seal.
9. Place the prepared Besbarmak on a baking sheet.
10. Bake for 15-20 minutes or until the dumplings are golden brown.

# ZHENT (HONEY AND NUT DESSERT)

- **Servings:** 6
- **Time:** 30 minutes

**Ingredients:**

- 1 cup mixed nuts (walnuts, almonds, hazelnuts), chopped
- 1/2 cup honey
- 1/4 cup unsalted butter
- 1/2 teaspoon ground cinnamon
- 1/4 teaspoon ground cardamom
- 1/4 teaspoon vanilla extract
- Pinch of salt

**Instructions:**

1. In a dry pan over medium heat, toast the chopped nuts until fragrant and lightly browned. Remove from heat and set aside.
2. In a saucepan, melt the unsalted butter over low heat.
3. Add honey, ground cinnamon, ground cardamom, vanilla extract, and a pinch of salt to the melted butter. Stir well to combine.
4. Bring the honey mixture to a gentle simmer, allowing it to bubble for 2-3 minutes.
5. Add the toasted nuts to the honey mixture, stirring to coat the nuts evenly.
6. Continue to cook for an additional 2-3 minutes, ensuring the nuts are well-coated with the honey mixture.
7. Remove the pan from heat and let the Zhent mixture cool slightly.
8. While still warm, shape the Zhent into small clusters or bars using your hands or a mold.
9. Allow the Zhent to cool completely and firm up.

# BAURSAK (FRIED DOUGH BALLS)

- **Servings: 6**

- **Time:** 2 hours

**Ingredients:**

- 3 cups all-purpose flour
- 1 cup warm milk
- 1 tablespoon vegetable oil
- 1 tablespoon sugar
- 1 tablespoon active dry yeast
- 1/2 teaspoon salt
- Vegetable oil for frying

**Instructions:**

1. In a bowl, combine warm milk, sugar, and active dry yeast. Let it sit for 5-10 minutes until frothy.
2. In a large mixing bowl, combine flour, vegetable oil, salt, and the yeast mixture. Knead into a soft dough. Cover and let it rise for 1 hour.
3. After the dough has risen, heat vegetable oil in a deep fryer or a large, deep pan to 350°F (175°C).
4. Divide the dough into small balls, approximately 1-2 inches in diameter.
5. Roll out each ball into a small disc or shape of your preference.
6. Carefully place the dough into the hot oil and fry until golden brown on both sides, turning as needed.
7. Remove the fried dough balls with a slotted spoon and place them on paper towels to absorb excess oil.
8. Repeat the process with the remaining dough balls.
9. Serve the Baursak warm as a delightful snack or side dish.

# CHALAP (FRIED MILK DOUGH)

- **Servings:** 6
- **Time:** 2 hours

**Ingredients:**

- 3 cups all-purpose flour
- 1 cup warm milk
- 2 tablespoons vegetable oil
- 1 tablespoon sugar
- 1 tablespoon active dry yeast
- 1/2 teaspoon salt
- Vegetable oil for frying

**Instructions:**

1. In a bowl, combine warm milk, sugar, and active dry yeast. Let it sit for 5-10 minutes until frothy.
2. In a large mixing bowl, combine flour, vegetable oil, salt, and the yeast mixture. Knead into a soft dough. Cover and let it rise for 1 hour.
3. After the dough has risen, heat vegetable oil in a deep fryer or a large, deep pan to 350°F (175°C).
4. Divide the dough into small balls, approximately 1-2 inches in diameter.
5. Roll out each ball into a thin disc or shape of your preference.
6. Carefully place the dough into the hot oil and fry until golden brown on both sides, turning as needed.
7. Remove the fried milk dough with a slotted spoon and place it on paper towels to absorb excess oil.
8. Repeat the process with the remaining dough balls.

9. Serve the Chalap warm as a delightful snack or dessert.

# SARY GOGEL (SWEET PASTRY WITH HONEY)

- **Servings:** 6
- **Time:** 2 hours

**Ingredients:** *For the Dough:*

- 3 cups all-purpose flour
- 1 cup warm milk
- 1/4 cup vegetable oil
- 1 tablespoon sugar
- 1 tablespoon active dry yeast
- 1/2 teaspoon salt

*For the Honey Glaze:*

- 1/2 cup honey
- 2 tablespoons unsalted butter
- 1 teaspoon vanilla extract

**Instructions:** *For the Dough:*

1. In a bowl, combine warm milk, sugar, and active dry yeast. Let it sit for 5-10 minutes until frothy.
2. In a large mixing bowl, combine flour, vegetable oil, salt, and the yeast mixture. Knead into a soft dough. Cover and let it rise for 1 hour.
3. After the dough has risen, preheat the oven to 375°F (190°C).

4. Divide the dough into small balls and roll each ball into a thin oval or round shape.
5. Place the rolled dough on a baking sheet.

*For the Honey Glaze:* 6. In a small saucepan, melt unsalted butter and honey over low heat. Stir in vanilla extract.

7. Brush the honey glaze over each rolled dough, ensuring an even coating.
8. Bake in the preheated oven for 15-20 minutes or until the pastries are golden brown.
9. Remove from the oven and let the Sary Gogel cool slightly.

# KYRGYZ HALVA (NUT AND SEED DESSERT)

- **Servings:** 8
- **Time:** 1 hour

**Ingredients:**

- 1 cup sunflower seeds
- 1 cup pumpkin seeds
- 1 cup almonds, blanched and chopped
- 1 cup walnuts, chopped
- 1 cup sesame seeds
- 1 cup honey
- 1 cup sugar
- 1/2 cup water
- 1/2 teaspoon ground cardamom
- 1/2 teaspoon vanilla extract
- A pinch of salt

## Instructions:

1. In a dry pan over medium heat, toast sunflower seeds, pumpkin seeds, almonds, and walnuts until fragrant. Stir occasionally to prevent burning. Once toasted, set aside.
2. In the same pan, toast sesame seeds until golden brown. Set aside.
3. In a large mixing bowl, combine the toasted sunflower seeds, pumpkin seeds, almonds, walnuts, and sesame seeds.
4. In a saucepan, combine honey, sugar, water, ground cardamom, vanilla extract, and a pinch of salt. Stir over medium heat until the sugar dissolves.
5. Bring the honey mixture to a boil and cook until it reaches the soft-ball stage (about 235°F or 113°C).
6. Pour the hot honey syrup over the mixed nuts and seeds. Quickly stir to coat the nuts and seeds evenly with the syrup.
7. Transfer the mixture to a greased pan or mold, pressing it down firmly to create an even layer.
8. Allow the Kyrgyz Halva to cool and set at room temperature for a few hours or in the refrigerator.
9. Once set, cut the halva into squares or diamonds.

# TOKOCH (SWEET BREAD PUDDING)

- **Servings:** 6
- **Time:** 1.5 hours

## Ingredients:

- 6 slices stale bread, torn into small pieces
- 2 cups milk

- 3/4 cup sugar
- 3 large eggs
- 1/4 cup unsalted butter, melted
- 1 teaspoon vanilla extract
- 1/2 cup raisins (optional)
- A pinch of salt
- Ground cinnamon for dusting

**Instructions:**

1. Preheat the oven to 350°F (175°C). Grease a baking dish.
2. In a mixing bowl, soak the torn bread pieces in milk for about 15-20 minutes until the bread absorbs the milk.
3. In a separate bowl, beat the eggs and sugar together until well combined.
4. Add the melted butter, vanilla extract, and a pinch of salt to the egg and sugar mixture. Mix thoroughly.
5. Combine the soaked bread and egg mixture. If using raisins, fold them into the mixture.
6. Pour the bread pudding mixture into the greased baking dish.
7. Bake in the preheated oven for 45-50 minutes or until the top is golden brown and a toothpick inserted into the center comes out clean.
8. Remove from the oven and let it cool for a few minutes.
9. Dust the top with ground cinnamon for added flavor.
10. Serve warm, either as is or with a dollop of whipped cream or a drizzle of honey.

# MEASUREMENT CONVERSIONS

## Volume Conversions:

- 1 cup = 8 fluid ounces = 240 milliliters
- 1 tablespoon = 3 teaspoons = 15 milliliters
- 1 fluid ounce = 2 tablespoons = 30 milliliters
- 1 quart = 4 cups = 32 fluid ounces = 946 milliliters
- 1 gallon = 4 quarts = 128 fluid ounces = 3.78 liters
- 1 liter = 1,000 milliliters = 33.8 fluid ounces
- 1 milliliter = 0.034 fluid ounces = 0.002 cups

## Weight Conversions:

- 1 pound = 16 ounces = 453.592 grams
- 1 ounce = 28.349 grams
- 1 gram = 0.035 ounces = 0.001 kilograms
- 1 kilogram = 1,000 grams = 35.274 ounces = 2.205 pounds

## Temperature Conversions:

- To convert from Fahrenheit to Celsius: (°F - 32) / 1.8
- To convert from Celsius to Fahrenheit: (°C * 1.8) + 32

## Length Conversions:

- 1 inch = 2.54 centimeters
- 1 foot = 12 inches = 30.48 centimeters
- 1 yard = 3 feet = 36 inches = 91.44 centimeters
- 1 meter = 100 centimeters = 1.094 yards.

Printed in Great Britain
by Amazon

41731792R00046